THE
INNER PLANETS
MERCURY, VENUS, AND MARS

THE INNER PLANETS
MERCURY, VENUS, AND MARS

Edited by Sherman Hollar

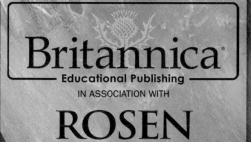

Britannica
Educational Publishing

IN ASSOCIATION WITH

ROSEN
EDUCATIONAL SERVICES

Published in 2012 by Britannica Educational Publishing
(a trademark of Encyclopædia Britannica, Inc.)
in association with Rosen Educational Services, LLC
29 East 21st Street, New York, NY 10010.

Distributed exclusively by Rosen Educational Services.
For a listing of additional Britannica Educational Publishing titles, call toll free (800) 237-9932.

First Edition

Britannica Educational Publishing
Michael I. Levy: Executive Editor, Encyclopædia Britannica
J.E. Luebering: Director, Core Reference Group, Encyclopædia Britannica
Adam Augustyn: Assistant Manager, Encyclopædia Britannica

Anthony L. Green: Editor, Compton's by Britannica
Michael Anderson: Senior Editor, Compton's by Britannica
Sherman Hollar: Associate Editor, Compton's by Britannica

Marilyn L. Barton: Senior Coordinator, Production Control
Steven Bosco: Director, Editorial Technologies
Lisa S. Braucher: Senior Producer and Data Editor
Yvette Charboneau: Senior Copy Editor
Kathy Nakamura: Manager, Media Acquisition

Rosen Educational Services
Alexandra Hanson-Harding: Editor
Nelson Sá: Art Director
Cindy Reiman: Photography Manager
Matthew Cauli: Designer, Cover Design
Introduction by Alexandra Hanson-Harding

Library of Congress Cataloging-in-Publication Data

The inner planets : Mercury, Venus, and Mars / edited by Sherman Hollar.
    p. cm. — (The solar system)
"In association with Britannica Educational Publishing, Rosen Educational Services."
Includes bibliographical references and index.
ISBN 978-1-61530-512-4 (lib. bd.)
1. Inner planets—Juvenile literature. 2. Mercury (Planet)—Juvenile literature. 3. Venus (Planet)—
Juvenile literature. 4. Mars (Planet)—Juvenile literature. I. Hollar, Sherman.
QB602.I56 2012
523.4—dc22

                                                                          2010053891

Manufactured in the United States of America

On the front cover, page 3: Illustration of Mars created by computer. *Shutterstock.com*

Cover (top), back cover, pp. 3 (top), 16, 17, 26, 27, 32, 39, 59, 60, 74, 75 Shutterstock.com; pp. 10, 19, 28, 35, 53, 62, 87, 88, 90, 92, 93 © www.istockphoto.com/Spectral-Design; remaining interior background image © www.istockphoto.com/Sergii Tsololo

CONTENTS

Since ancient times, humans have gazed in wonder at the vast blanket of stars covering the night sky. Records going back 5,000 years show that ancient Sumerian astronomers recognized that some "stars" moved differently than other celestial bodies. Three special objects they tracked are the three closest planets to Earth: Mercury, Venus, and Mars. These objects still fascinate today. This book will take you on a journey to learn about our neighbors in the solar system.

The first stop on our tour will be tiny Mercury. At less than two-fifths Earth's size, it is the smallest of the eight planets. Because it is the closest planet to the Sun, it can complete an orbit around the Sun in only 88 Earth days. But it takes almost 59 Earth days to complete one rotation about its axis. Mercury has almost no atmosphere, leaving its dry and rocky surface little protection from crater blasts by asteroids. Mercury is the densest planet in the solar system.

Our second stop is Venus, the solar system's third smallest planet and the one most similar in size to Earth. Venus' atmosphere is remarkably massive. Made mostly of thick, heat-trapping layers of carbon dioxide, the heavy atmosphere makes it the hottest planet in the solar system. This thick atmosphere has also made it difficult to study the planet's surface. Venus' orbit and rotation are also unusual. A year on Venus is 225 days. But the planet spins about its axis very slowly, completing one rotation about every 243 Earth days—making Venus the only planet in the solar system that takes longer to rotate once about its axis than to travel once around the Sun. Venus and Uranus are also the only two planets that rotate counterclockwise.

The third stop on our journey, Mars, the second smallest planet in the solar system, is only about half Earth's size. The planet completes one revolution around the Sun in about 687 Earth days. A Martian day lasts a little longer than 24 hours. It also has two small potato-shaped moons. Observers have long wondered if there was life on Mars because it appears as if there are channels that might once have contained water, a necessary ingredient for life. In fact, there still is water on Mars, but most of it is frozen beneath the planet's surface. The thin atmosphere doesn't shield the surface from harsh ultraviolet radiation or from being hit by space junk.

Since the beginning of the space age, humans have had the power to do more than

Telescopic observers have noted distinctive bright and dark features on Mars for hundreds of years. One of the sharpest images taken from the vicinity of Earth, photographed by the Hubble Space Telescope, captures the red planet on the last day of spring in the northern hemisphere. The large dark marking just below and to the east of center is Syrtis Major. Beneath it is the giant impact basin Hellas, covered with an oval of white clouds. **NASA/JPL/David Crisp and the WFPC2 Science Team**

study the inner planets from afar. The development of space probes and satellites has allowed us to send spacecraft to fly by and even land on these planets. Such missions have resulted in a number of discoveries. For instance, we now know that Mercury shrank considerably as it cooled early in its history and that Venus, though sizzlingly hot and dry today, probably once had oceans. And though we have yet to find signs of life on Mars, much evidence has been collected suggesting that Mars was once more Earth-like, with warmer temperatures as well as flowing water. Even now, space missions continue. In 2011 NASA's Messenger probe is thoroughly exploring Mercury, for instance. As you read this book, you will get a sense of what humans have learned so far about our three neighboring planets—and what we still have to discover.

CHARACTERISTICS OF MERCURY

The planet that orbits closest to the Sun is Mercury. It is also the smallest of the eight planets in the solar system. These features make Mercury difficult to view from Earth, as the small planet rises and sets within about two hours of the Sun. Observers on Earth can only ever see the planet during twilight, when the Sun is just below the horizon. Relatively little was known about Mercury until the Mariner 10 spacecraft visited it in 1974–75. It was more than 30 years before another spacecraft, Messenger, visited the planet.

Mercury's orbit lies between the Sun and the orbit of Venus. Along with Venus, Earth, and Mars, Mercury is one of the inner planets nearest to the Sun. The inner planets are also known as the terrestrial, or Earth-like, planets. They are dense, rocky bodies that are much smaller than the solar system's outer planets. Mercury has no known moons.

SIZE, MASS, AND DENSITY

Mercury is the smallest planet in both mass and diameter. It is about 18 times less massive

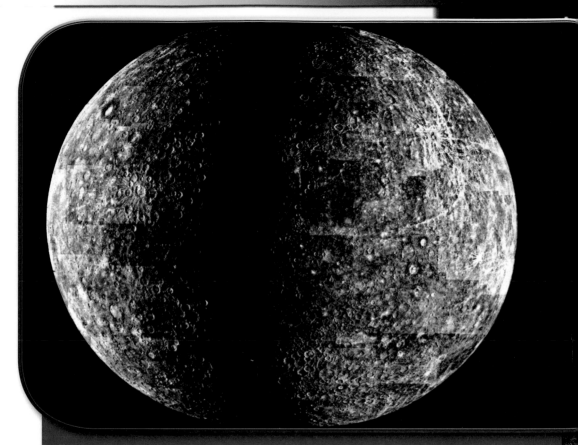

Each view of the planet Mercury is a mosaic of many images taken by the Mariner 10 spacecraft during its first flyby of the planet in March 1974. Each view shows about half of the hemisphere that was in sunlight at the time. NASA/JPLNASA/JPL

than Earth. With a diameter of about 3,032 miles (4,879 kilometers), Mercury is not quite two-fifths the size of Earth. It is only about a third larger than Earth's Moon. In fact, two moons in the solar system—Jupiter's moon Ganymede and Saturn's moon Titan—are larger than Mercury. However, Mercury is larger than the dwarf planet Pluto. For some 75 years, when Pluto was classified as a planet, Mercury was considered the second-smallest planet.

Mercury is the densest planet in the solar system, followed by Earth (if one takes into account the planets' internal compression because of gravity). Mercury is unusually dense because it is composed of a high percentage of metal. The metal is concentrated in a comparatively huge core, which accounts for nearly 75 percent of Mercury's diameter.

APPEARANCE FROM EARTH

Mercury can be seen from Earth without a telescope. It always appears close to the Sun (within about 28 angular degrees). For this reason, the planet can only be seen near the horizon. At certain times of the year it appears as a "morning star" just before sunrise, while at other times it appears as an "evening star" just after sunset.

Because Mercury's orbit lies between Earth's orbit and the Sun, Mercury displays phases like those of the Moon and the planet Venus. These phases can only be seen with the aid of a telescope. Mercury sometimes

Five separate images were combined to show Mercury crossing in front of the Sun during a type of eclipse called a transit on Nov. 15, 1999. The false-color images were taken in ultraviolet light by the Transition Region and Coronal Explorer (TRACE) satellite in Earth's orbit. The time between successive images was about seven minutes. **NASA/ TRACE/SMEX**

looks like a crescent to observers on Earth. At other times, when Mercury and Earth are in different positions, more of the sunlight reflected off Mercury can be seen from Earth. Mercury then appears as a half or fuller disk.

About a dozen times each century, Mercury passes directly between Earth and the Sun. This event, called a transit, is a type of eclipse. During a transit of Mercury, the planet appears as a small black disk against the background of the bright Sun. Binoculars or a small telescope, safely equipped with a solar filter, are required to observe a transit, preferably by projection of the Sun's image onto a white card. The next transit of Mercury is in 2016.

ORBIT AND SPIN

On average, Mercury orbits the Sun at a distance of nearly 36 million miles (58 million kilometers). Like all the planets, it travels around the Sun in an elliptical (oval-shaped) orbit. Mercury's orbit is the most eccentric, or elongated, of all the planets. Its orbit is also the most tilted. The plane of Mercury's orbit is tipped about 7 degrees relative to the ecliptic, or the plane of Earth's orbit. Mercury completes one orbit around the Sun about every 88 Earth days. In other words, one year on Mercury lasts some 88 Earth days.

The planet was named after the ancient Roman god Mercury, the counterpart of the ancient Greek god Hermes. Like Hermes, the swift-footed messenger of the gods, the planet Mercury is known for the speed with which it moves across the sky. The planet circles the Sun at an average rate of about 30 miles (48 kilometers) per second, the fastest of the eight planets.

Numerous craters and impact basins mark the surface of Mercury. An image taken by a space probe called the Messenger during its first flyby in January 2008 shows part of the planet. NASA/Johns Hopkins University Applied Physics Laboratory/Carnegie Institution of Washington

Although Mercury moves along its orbit very quickly, it spins slowly. It takes almost 59 Earth days to complete one rotation about its axis. Mercury rotates on its axis only three times for every two revolutions it makes around the Sun. The combination of a slow spin and a fast orbit leads to an

ORBITS OF THE PLANETS

Like the other seven planets, Mercury orbits the Sun in a counterclockwise direction—the same direction as the Sun's rotation. The planets also orbit in nearly the same plane, so that their paths trace out a large disk around the Sun's equator. The orbital planes of most of the eight planets are within about 3.5 degrees of the ecliptic plane, or the plane in which Earth orbits. As mentioned earlier, however, Mercury's orbit is inclined about 7 degrees relative to the ecliptic plane.

In the early 1600s German astronomer Johannes Kepler discovered three major laws that govern the motions of the planets. The first law describes the shape of their orbits, which are not exactly circular but slightly oval, or elliptical. Mercury has the most eccentric orbit of the planets, while Venus and Neptune have the most circular orbits.

Kepler's second law describes the velocities (speeds) of the planets in their orbits. It states that an imaginary line drawn from a planet to the Sun sweeps across equal areas in equal periods of time. This means that the planets move faster when their orbits bring them closer to the Sun and more slowly when they are farther away. It takes much more time for Uranus to orbit the Sun than Mercury, for instance. Kepler's third law allows one to calculate a planet's orbital period, or the time it takes the planet to complete one orbit around the Sun, if one knows its average distance from the Sun, and vice versa. The law states that the square of a planet's orbital period is proportional to the cube of the planet's average distance from the Sun.

unusual situation. A day on Mercury—the time it takes for the Sun to appear straight overhead, to set, and then to rise straight overhead again—lasts about 176 Earth days. So on Mercury a day is twice as long as a year.

This characteristic, combined with Mercury's highly eccentric orbit, creates some strange effects. The planet's distance from the Sun varies greatly as it travels along its orbit. The farthest Mercury gets from the Sun is about 43 million miles (70 million kilometers). At that point in the planet's orbit, an observer on Mercury would see the Sun appear about twice as large as it does from Earth. The closest Mercury gets to the Sun is some 29 million miles (46 million kilometers). The Sun would at that point appear some three times as large as it does from Earth. Even more unusually, the Sun would not seem to move steadily across Mercury's sky. Its apparent speed would change depending on the viewer's location on the planet and on the planet's distance from the Sun. The Sun would sometimes even appear to briefly reverse its course.

Mercury's spin axis is very nearly perpendicular, or upright, relative to its plane of orbit. By comparison, Earth's axis is tilted almost 24 degrees. This inclination is the main reason there are seasons on Earth. Because Mercury's axis is not tilted, it does not have Earth-like seasons.

PHYSICAL FEATURES AND EXPLORATION OF MERCURY

Mercury has been known for approximately 5,000 years. As mentioned in chapter one, its closeness to the Sun makes it difficult to observe from Earth. Moreover, the Hubble Space Telescope and other Earth-orbiting instruments are too sensitive to be pointed that close to the Sun. Astronomers have used radar to study Mercury by sending radio waves toward the planet and detecting and measuring the waves that bounce back.

ATMOSPHERE

Unlike the other planets, Mercury has no significant atmosphere, or surrounding layers of gases. At Mercury's surface, the pressure—the force exerted by the atmosphere—is less than one-trillionth that at Earth's surface. Mercury's extremely thin layer of gases includes atoms of helium, hydrogen, oxygen, and sodium. The gases do not remain near the planet long before the Sun's heat blasts them away. They are replenished partly by the solar wind, the flow of charged particles from the Sun. Other gases come from asteroids and comets and from the planet's surface.

Mercury has a magnetic field similar in form to Earth's. However, Mercury's magnetic field is much weaker, at only about 1 percent the strength of Earth's.

Temperatures on Mercury vary widely. Its closeness to the Sun makes it a broiling-hot world by day, with daytime surface temperatures exceeding 800 °F (430 °C) at parts of the planet. Because Mercury lacks a thick atmosphere to trap heat, however, the planet cools greatly at night. The temperature can drop to about - 300 °F (- 180 °C) just before dawn. The average surface temperature is about 332 °F (167 °C).

SURFACE

Mercury's surface is dry and rocky. Much of it is heavily cratered, somewhat like Earth's Moon. Impact craters form when meteorites, asteroids, or comets crash into a rocky planet or similar body, scarring the surface. Planetary scientists can estimate the age of a surface by the number of impact craters on it. In general, the more craters a surface has, the older it is. Mercury's heavily cratered surfaces are probably ancient.

Between the planet's heavily cratered regions are areas of flat and gently rolling plains with fewer craters. Elsewhere there are smooth, flat plains with very few craters.

A double-ringed crater on Mercury appears at left in an image taken by the Messenger spacecraft on Jan. 14, 2008. After the crater formed, it was apparently filled in with smooth plains material, perhaps volcanic lava. A long scarp, or cliff, runs along part of its rim and also cuts through another crater at bottom right. NASA/Johns Hopkins University Applied Physics Laboratory/Carnegie Institution of Washington

Volcanic lava flows probably smoothed the surfaces of these plains.

Impacts have formed craters on Mercury of all different sizes. The planet also has several huge impact basins. Each of these basins has multiple rings in a bull's-eye pattern. The most prominent impact basin, named Caloris, measures about 900 miles (1,550 kilometers) across. Caloris is one of the youngest and largest impact features in the solar system. Along the rim of the basin, mountains rise to heights of nearly 1.9 miles (3 kilometers). On the opposite side of the planet from Caloris is an area of strange hilly terrain. Planetary scientists think it resulted from the same impact that created the Caloris basin. The crash caused seismic waves (vibrations) to ripple through the planet. The waves came to a focus on the part of Mercury opposite the crash site, where they warped the terrain.

Hundreds of long, steep cliffs called scarps also mark the planet's surface. Planetary scientists believe that, at some point in Mercury's history, part of the planet's interior (the mantle) began to cool and shrink. As the planet shrank, the crust buckled and cracked, forming the many scarps. Mercury may even still be shrinking.

The side of Mercury directly opposite the Caloris impact basin has an area of oddly contorted and hilly terrain, which appears in an image taken by the Mariner 10 spacecraft. Seismic waves from the impact that formed Caloris traveled around the planet and warped the terrain on the opposite side. The smooth interior of the large crater at left indicates that its floor filled in sometime after the impact. **NASA/JPL**

INTERIOR

Like Earth, Mercury has three separate layers: a metallic core at the center, a middle rocky layer called a mantle, and a thin rocky crust. In both planets, the core is made mostly of iron. However, Mercury's core is proportionally much larger than Earth's. The core takes up about 42 percent of Mercury's volume, compared with only

about 16 percent for Earth. This accounts for Mercury's great density.

OBSERVATION AND EXPLORATION

The planet's nearness to the Sun presents challenges for space probes, which must contend with great heat and the enormous pull of the Sun's gravity. A spacecraft needs a lot of energy in order to enter into orbit around Mercury.

Much of the information known about Mercury comes from images and data transmitted by the Mariner 10 spacecraft, the first to visit the planet. The National Aeronautics and Space Administration (NASA) launched the craft in November 1973 toward Venus for the initial leg of its mission. Mariner 10 became the first spacecraft to use a "gravity assist," drawing on Venus' gravitational field to boost its speed and divert its course toward Mercury. It captured the first close-up photographs of Mercury in March 1974. Mariner 10 encountered Mercury twice more. Its final and closest pass, in

NASA technicians carefully lift the Messenger spacecraft in order to move it to a prelaunch testing stand. NASA

NASA's Messenger Probe

Messenger was launched on Aug. 3, 2004, by a Delta II rocket from Cape Canaveral, Fla. Its first flybys were of Earth, on Aug. 2, 2005, and of Venus, on Oct. 24, 2006, and June 5, 2007. Flybys of Mercury happened on Jan. 14 and Oct. 6, 2008, and on Sept. 29, 2009. A fourth encounter began early in 2011, when a thruster maneuver inserted Messenger into orbit around Mercury where it will study the planet closely for a year, using sophisticated equipment. The spacecraft's nominal mission will end in 2012.

The Messenger mission was designed to answer a number of major scientific questions. Among them are: Why is Mercury so dense?

Artist's impression of the Messenger spacecraft near the planet Mercury. NASA/Johns Hopkins University Applied Physics Laboratory/ Carnegie Institution of Washington

What is the geologic history of Mercury? What is the nature of Mercury's magnetic field? And what is the structure of Mercury's core?

Messenger has already made a number of discoveries. During its first flyby of Mercury, Messenger revealed that the planet's craters are only half as deep as those of the Moon. The Caloris impact basin was found to have evidence of volcanic vents. Messenger also discovered huge cliffs at the top of crustal faults called lobate scarps. These structures indicate that the planet, as it cooled early in its history, shrank by a third more than what had previously been believed.

March 1975, brought it to within 200 miles (325 kilometers) of the surface.

Mariner 10's orbital path allowed it to photograph only one side of Mercury. Low-resolution radar images taken from Earth suggested that the planet's other hemisphere has broadly similar terrain; this was confirmed when the Messenger spacecraft photographed areas of the surface unseen by Mariner. NASA launched Messenger, only the second spacecraft ever sent to Mercury, in 2004. It was designed to be the first probe to orbit the planet, getting gravity assists during a flyby of Earth, two flybys of Venus, and three flybys of Mercury.

chapter 3

CHARACTERISTICS OF VENUS

The second planet from the Sun is Venus. After the Moon, Venus is the most brilliant natural object in the nighttime sky. It is the closest planet to Earth, and it is also the most similar to Earth in size, mass, volume, and density. These similarities suggest that the two planets may have had similar histories. Scientists are thus intrigued by the question of why Venus and Earth are now so different.

Venus was named after the ancient Roman goddess of love and beauty, but its conditions are anything but hospitable and inviting to humans. Unlike Earth, Venus is extremely hot and dry. The planet is always shrouded by a thick layer of clouds. Venus has a massive atmosphere, or surrounding layers of gases, composed mainly of carbon dioxide. This thick atmosphere traps heat, making Venus the hottest planet in the solar system.

The permanent blanket of clouds also makes it difficult to study the planet. Little was known about the surface and atmosphere until the 1960s, when astronomers made the first radar observations of Venus

Scientists use radar to pierce the thick clouds shrouding Venus and "see" the surface below. An image generated by computer from radar data collected by the Magellan spacecraft shows the surface of the northern hemisphere. **NASA/JPL/Caltech (NASA photo # PIA00271)**

and unmanned spacecraft began visiting the planet. Venus' orbit lies between the orbits of Mercury and Earth. Like Mercury, Venus has no known moon.

SIZE, MASS, AND DENSITY

Venus is the third smallest planet in the solar system, after Mercury and Mars. It is a near twin of Earth in size, mass, and density. Venus' diameter is about 7,521 miles (12,104

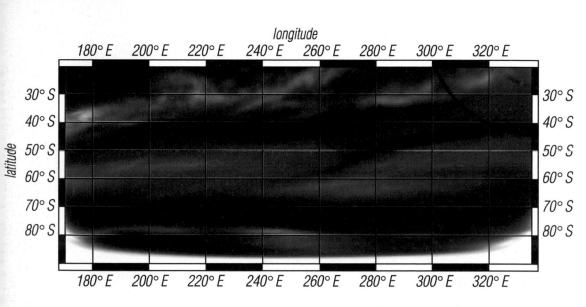

An infrared image taken by the Venus Express orbiter shows wind-blown clouds in the night sky above Venus. **ESA/VIRTIS/INAF-IASF/Obs. de Paris-LEIA**

kilometers), compared with some 7,926 miles (12,756 kilometers) for Earth. Its mass is approximately 80 percent of Earth's, and its density is about 95 percent of Earth's. The surface gravity of the two planets is also of similar strength.

APPEARANCE FROM EARTH

Along with Mercury, Venus is an "inferior" planet, or one whose orbit is smaller than Earth's. For this reason, Venus always appears in Earth's sky in roughly the same direction as the Sun. At some times of the year the planet can be seen as a "morning star," appearing in the hours before sunrise. At other times it can be seen as an "evening star" in the hours after sunset. Venus often can be seen in clear skies during daylight, if the observer knows exactly where to look.

Because Venus orbits closer to the Sun than Earth does, it exhibits phase changes as viewed from Earth. These phases are similar to those of the Moon and Mercury. Venus sometimes appears as a thin crescent and sometimes as a half or fuller disk. It passes through one cycle of phases about every 584 Earth days. The phases can be seen easily in high-power binoculars or a small telescope.

TRANSITS OF VENUS

Transits of Venus are rare, but when they do happen, they occur in December and June. Transits of Venus generally follow a recurrence pattern of 8, 121, 8, and 105 years before starting over. Following the transits of Dec. 9, 1874, and Dec. 6, 1882, the world waited 121 years until June 8, 2004, for the next transit to occur. Dates for successive transits of Venus are June 6, 2012, and, after a 105-year interval, Dec. 11, 2117, and Dec. 8, 2125. Unlike a transit of Mercury, a transit of Venus can be watched without magnification through a suitable dark filter or as an image projected on a screen through a pinhole lens.

Observing the transits of Venus was of great importance to 18th- and 19th-century astronomers because careful timings of the events permitted accurate measurement of the distance between Venus and Earth. This distance in turn allowed calculation of the distance between Earth and the Sun, called the astronomical unit, as well as the distances to the Sun of all the other planets.

Venus rarely but regularly passes directly between Earth and the Sun. During this event, or transit, the planet appears to observers on Earth as a small black disk crossing the bright disk of the Sun. Two transits of Venus occur about every 125 years. The transits occur in pairs eight years apart.

ORBIT AND SPIN

Venus' orbit is the most nearly circular of all the planets. It orbits the Sun at a mean distance of about 67 million miles (108 million kilometers). This is about 30 percent closer to the Sun than Earth's orbit is. At its closest approach to Earth, Venus is about 26 million miles (42 million kilometers) away; at its farthest, Venus is some 160 million miles (257 million kilometers) away. Venus completes one orbital revolution about every 225 Earth days, which is the length of one year on Venus.

Venus' rotation is unusual in a couple of ways. It spins about its axis very slowly, completing one rotation about every 243 Earth days. It is the only planet in the solar system that takes longer to rotate once about its axis than to travel once around the Sun. These two motions combine so that a day on Venus—the time it takes for the Sun to appear straight overhead, to set, and then to rise straight overhead again—lasts about 117 Earth days.

Because of its slow rotation, Venus is more nearly spherical than Earth and most other planets. The force from a planet's rotation generally causes some bulging at the equator and flattening at the poles. These distortions are minimized on Venus.

Venus also rotates in retrograde motion, or the direction opposite that of most of the other planets and members of the solar system. Six of the eight planets rotate clockwise when viewed from above the northern pole, while only Venus and Uranus rotate counterclockwise. To an observer on Venus, the Sun would appear to rise in the west and set in the east (if one could see through the thick clouds). Venus' spin axis is tilted only about 3 degrees relative to the plane of its orbit. This means that seasonal variations on the planet are probably very slight.

Unlike Earth and most of the other planets, Venus does not have a global magnetic field. This might result from its extremely slow rotation rate. Scientists think that a planet's rotation helps drive the fluid motions in the planet's core that generate a magnetic field.

PHYSICAL FEATURES AND EXPLORATION OF VENUS

S cientists today use radar to pierce the thick clouds shrouding Venus to "see" the surface below. Exploration of the planet with spacecraft, which began in the 1960s, also has played a crucial role in increasing our knowledge of Venus.

ATMOSPHERE

Venus has by far the most massive atmosphere of the four terrestrial planets. The pressure exerted by the atmosphere at the planet's surface is about 95 bars, or 95 times the atmospheric pressure at sea level on Earth. It is composed of more than 96 percent carbon dioxide and about 3.5 percent molecular nitrogen, with only trace amounts of other gases.

The layer of clouds that perpetually blankets Venus is very thick. The main cloud deck rises from an altitude of about 30 miles (48 kilometers) to nearly 42 miles (68 kilometers). In addition, thin hazes extend several miles above and below the main deck. The clouds are made of microscopic particles, predominantly droplets of sulfuric acid. The clouds may also contain solid crystals. Some cloud-top regions appear dark in ultraviolet light. This might indicate the presence of sulfur dioxide, chlorine, or solid sulfur.

Although Venus rotates slowly (once in 243 days), the atmosphere circulates surprisingly

Large v-shaped bands in Venus' clouds are revealed in a photograph taken in ultraviolet light by the Pioneer Venus 1 spacecraft. Although the planet's cloud cover is nearly featureless in visible light, ultraviolet imaging shows a distinctive structure and pattern. Color was added to the image to emulate Venus' yellow-white appearance to the eye. **NASA/JPL**

Venus' middle and lower atmosphere

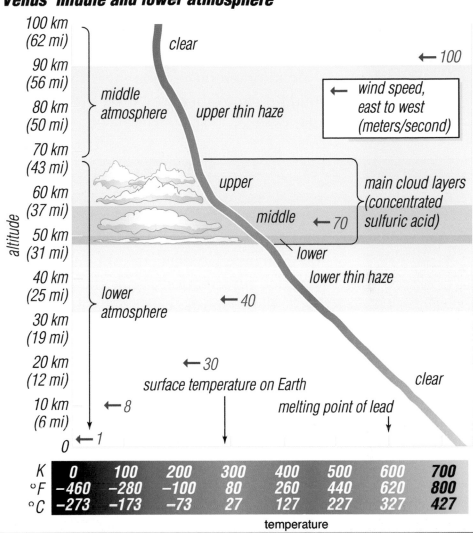

A graph shows temperatures and pressures at different levels in Venus's lower and middle atmosphere, up to an altitude of 100 kilometers (62 miles). The data are based on measurements made by the Pioneer Venus mission's atmospheric probes and other spacecrafts. Red arrows indicate wind speeds. Encyclopædia Britannica, Inc.

rapidly. At cloud level the atmosphere completely circles the planet every four days. Wind speeds vary widely according to the altitude. Winds range from about 220 miles (360 kilometers) per hour near the top of the middle atmosphere to only a slight breeze at the surface.

SURFACE

Venus has a dry, rocky surface. In the 1970s and '80s the Soviet Union's Venera series of unmanned spacecraft obtained the first detailed information about the planet's surface. Photographs taken by robotic Venera landers revealed plains strewn with flat, slabby rocks and a darker, fine-grained soil. Venera landers also measured the chemical composition of the surface at the landing sites. Their analysis suggested that the rock composition might be similar to basalts—volcanic rocks—found on the ocean floors of Earth.

Earth-based observatories and several orbiting spacecraft have mapped Venus' surface using radar. The radar maps reveal diverse and geologically complex surface terrain. Most of the planet consists of gently rolling plains. There are also several lowland areas and two continent-sized highlands:

VENUS AND THE GREENHOUSE EFFECT

Even though Venus is closer to the Sun than Earth is, Venus absorbs less sunlight than Earth does. Venus' thick clouds allow only a little light through. About 85 percent of the sunlight that strikes the clouds gets reflected back into space. The sunlight that does penetrate the clouds is absorbed by the lower atmosphere and surface. As the light heats the lower atmosphere and the ground, they radiate some of the energy back at longer, infrared wavelengths. On Earth most such energy escapes back into space. This keeps Earth's surface relatively cool. On Venus, however, the thick atmosphere traps much of the reradiated infrared energy.

This phenomenon, called the greenhouse effect, makes Venus extremely hot. The planet's average surface temperature is about 867 °F (464 °C), which is hot enough to melt lead. Venus is even hotter than Mercury, the planet closest to the Sun. The rocks on Venus may glow faintly red from their own heat.

Studying the greenhouse effect on Venus has given scientists an improved understanding of the more subtle but very important influence of greenhouse gases in Earth's atmosphere. (Rising levels of carbon dioxide, methane, and other so-called greenhouse gases in Earth's atmosphere are thought to be causing global warming on Earth by most climate scientists.)

Ishtar Terra and Aphrodite Terra. Ishtar is about the size of Australia, while Aphrodite is roughly the size of South America. Ishtar has a central plateau surrounded by mountains, including the enormous Maxwell Montes range. Its peaks rise to the highest elevations on Venus, about 7 miles (11 kilometers) above the planet's average surface elevation.

As on Earth, geologic activity has shaped the surface terrain. Upward and downward movements within Venus' outer shell have folded, fractured, and otherwise deformed the crust. Features that probably formed this way include mountain belts and rift valleys, or deep, narrow troughs. Another such type of terrain on Venus, called tessera, is very rugged, complex, and deformed. Tessera terrain typically has sets of parallel troughs and ridges that cut across one another at a wide range of angles. Hundreds of features called coronae are also found on the surface. A corona is a set of faults, fractures, and ridges in a circular or oval pattern. Some have a raised outer rim and a sagging center. Coronae probably form when blobs of molten material rise up in the planet's interior and distort the crust.

Many of Venus' surface features are associated with volcanic activity. The planet has more than a hundred shield volcanoes, and enormous fields of lava flows cover most of the rolling plains. There are also numerous small volcanic cones.

Like other planets, Venus has impact craters, which form when asteroids crash into

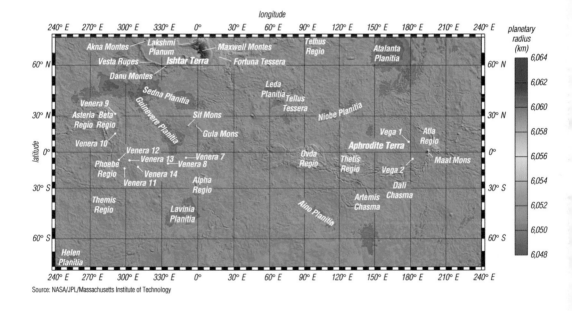

A surface map of Venus shows the planet's global topography. The map is color coded: The lowest elevations are in blue and the highest are in red. The elevation figures are expressed as distance from the center of the planet. **Encyclopædia Britannica, Inc.**

the surface. However, Venus does not have craters smaller than about a mile (1.5 kilometers). This is because the planet's thick atmosphere slows down and breaks apart smaller asteroids. Scientists can estimate the age of a solid planet's surface in part by analyzing its craters. In general, the more craters a surface has, the older it is. Venus

Venus's complex surface features include coronae. A false-color, computer-generated image based on radar data from the Magellan spacecraft shows a corona in an early stage, at left, characterized by raised crust, and a corona in a later stage, at right, in which the center has begun to sag. **Photo NASA/JPL/Caltech**

has comparatively few craters, and they are randomly distributed over the surface. This indicates that Venus' surface is in all places young for a planet. Scientists believe that Venus underwent an intense period of global resurfacing only roughly 500 million years ago. One possible explanation is that the planet's outer shell may have slowly

A shield volcano on Venus named Sif Mons appears in a computer-generated image based on radar data from the Magellan spacecraft. The volcano is about 1.2 miles (2 kilometers) high. **NASA/JPL**

thickened until eventually it collapsed. This may have been a single event or the last in a cycle of global convulsions that each time renewed the surface.

INTERIOR

What little is known about Venus' interior is mostly inferred from its similarity to Earth in terms of density and size. Planetary scientists theorize that Venus probably developed an interior roughly like that of Earth, with a metallic core and a rocky mantle and crust.

Venus' core probably extends outward about 1,860 miles (3,000 kilometers) from the planet's center. It likely contains iron and nickel like Earth's core. Venus' core probably also includes a less dense substance such as sulfur. Unlike most of the other planets, however, Venus has no magnetic field, so there is no direct evidence for a metallic core.

The mantle makes up the bulk of the planet. Gravitational data suggest that the crust is typically about 12–30 miles (20–50 kilometers) thick. It likely contains much basalt. As mentioned above, movements within Venus' mantle are thought to deform

the crust. These movements are mainly vertical. Venus does not now seem to experience plate tectonics as Earth does. Plate tectonics involves mainly horizontal movements of a planet's crust and upper mantle.

OBSERVATION AND EXPLORATION

Venus was observed from Earth for centuries before the invention of modern astronomical instruments. The Babylonians recorded its appearances in about 3000 BC, and ancient civilizations in China, Central America, Egypt, and Greece also observed the planet.

TELESCOPIC OBSERVATION

In the 17th century Galileo made the first telescopic observations of Venus. In 1610 he discovered the planet's phases. If Earth lay at the center of the solar system, as was then widely believed, Venus would not display such phases. Galileo's discovery was the first direct observational evidence to support Nicolaus Copernicus' then-controversial theory that Earth and the other planets orbit the Sun. Important telescopic observations were later made during the transits of Venus in the 1700s and 1800s.

When viewed through an optical (visible-light) telescope, Venus appears yellow-white and fairly featureless because of its permanent veil of clouds. Since the early 20th century astronomers have used wavelengths of light that lie outside the visible spectrum to uncover features of the planet that are otherwise hidden. Ultraviolet rays reveal swirls, v-shaped bands, and distinctive bright and dark markings in the clouds. Astronomers have used infrared radiation to study the composition of the atmosphere and clouds. Microwave studies have revealed the high temperatures at the planet's surface.

Radar studies have been particularly important to astronomers studying Venus. A large radio telescope outfitted with a transmitter can send out radio waves that pierce Venus' cloud screen and bounce off the planet's surface. The telescope then detects the returning radio waves.

SPACECRAFT EXPLORATION

More than 20 unmanned spacecraft have visited Venus, including craft that have flown by, orbited, and landed on the planet and that have sent probes parachuting through its atmosphere. Like Earth-based telescopes, spacecraft flying near Venus use radar to penetrate the deck of clouds and map the surface below. Missions to the surface have also had to contend with the planet's extremely high temperatures and pressures.

The United States Mariner and Soviet Venera missions were the first to successfully visit Venus. NASA launched the Mariner 2 spacecraft in August 1962. When it reached Venus a few months later, it became the first spacecraft to fly near another planet and return data. Approaching Venus within about 22,000 miles (35,000 kilometers), the craft surveyed the atmosphere and collected data about the planet's rotation and high surface temperatures and pressures. It found no evidence of a global magnetic field. In October 1967 Mariner 5 flew

The U.S. Mariner 5 spacecraft, shown being prepared for its launch on June 14, 1967, flew by Venus on Oct. 19, 1967. NASA

The Soviet Venera 4 atmospheric probe, shown on Earth before its launch, took direct measurements of Venus' atmosphere in 1967. It was the first object made by humans to enter the atmosphere of another planet and transmit data back to Earth. Tass/Sovfoto

closer to Venus, passing within about 2,500 miles (4,000 kilometers). Its more sensitive instruments returned more precise data about the atmosphere, including the heavy concentration of carbon dioxide. Mariner 10, the last craft of the series, took some 4,000 photographs of Venus during a flyby in 1974. It captured the first close-up ultraviolet images of Venus' clouds.

Another early NASA mission to the planet, called Pioneer Venus, included two craft. Pioneer Venus 1 and Pioneer Venus 2 arrived at the planet in December 1978. The first of these spacecraft orbited Venus for several years, collecting comprehensive data on the atmosphere. Its radar instrument produced the first high-quality map of Venus' surface topography. One of the longest-lived planetary spacecraft, Pioneer Venus 1 returned data for more than 14 years. Pioneer Venus 2, known as the Multiprobe, released four probes to collect data at different points in the planet's atmosphere.

Many Soviet missions targeted Venus from the 1960s to the 1980s. Several of the early missions failed, but the later Venera missions were outstanding successes. Venera 4 flew by Venus and released a probe into its atmosphere in October 1967. The probe was the

first human-made object to travel through the atmosphere of another planet and return data. It analyzed the chemical composition of Venus' upper atmosphere. In December 1970 Venera 7 became the first spacecraft to land on the surface of another planet and transmit data back to Earth. Veneras 9 and 10 each consisted of an orbiter and a lander. In October 1975 the orbiters became the first craft to orbit Venus, while the landers sent back close-up photographs of the surface. They were the first photographs taken from the surface of a planet other than Earth. The radar mappers aboard the final craft

The European Space Agency's Venus Express spacecraft and its launch rocket are shown prior to liftoff. ESA/ Starem — S. Corvaja

of the mission, Venera 15 and 16, produced high-quality images of the Venusian surface in 1983–84. Many of the types of geologic features found on Venus were first revealed by these twin orbiters.

In May 1989 NASA's Magellan became the first planetary spacecraft to be launched from a space shuttle. The craft surveyed Venus from August 1990 through October 1994. Its orbit carried it around the planet every three hours while it mapped the cloud-shrouded surface in great detail. The craft also made the first detailed map of Venus' gravitational field. Magellan found no evidence of plate tectonics on Venus, but it revealed data that suggest the planet is still geologically active at a couple of hot spots.

The first European mission to Venus was the orbiter Venus Express. The European Space Agency (ESA) launched the craft in November 2005. It began orbiting the planet in April 2006, with a camera, a visible-light and infrared imaging spectrometer, and other instruments on board to study the planet's magnetic field, plasma environment, atmosphere, and surface.

Venus Express observed small amounts of water and a large ratio of deuterium to hydrogen, both of which could be explained by the presence of oceans early in Venus' history. The spacecraft also returned the first images of cloud structures over the planet's south pole. Radio waves characteristic of lightning in Venus' clouds were discovered.

Venus Express completed its originally planned mission on July 24, 2007, but the mission was extended through December 2012. In recent years, Venus Express has also made numerous observations of Earth. These observations were intended to identify for astronomers the spectroscopic signatures of life on Earth that could possibly be seen on extrasolar planets (planets that orbit stars other than the Sun).

In addition to missions to Venus, several spacecraft have flown past Venus while on their way to other main targets. These flybys were designed as gravity assists, which transfer momentum from the planet to the spacecraft in order to increase the craft's velocity and adjust its course. Such gravity assists also allow spacecraft to investigate Venus while flying by. The first craft to use a gravity assist was Mariner 10, which flew past Venus in 1974 on its way to Mercury. Others have included NASA's Galileo, which flew by Venus in 1990 on its way to Jupiter, and NASA's Cassini, which flew by Venus in 1998 and 1999 on its way to Saturn.

CHARACTERISTICS OF MARS

The fourth planet from the Sun is Mars. Easily visible from Earth with the naked eye, it has intrigued stargazers since ancient times. It often appears quite bright and reddish in the night sky. Babylonians mentioned Mars in records from about 3,000 years ago, associating the blood-red planet with their god of death and disease. The name Mars is that of the ancient Roman god of war.

Mars is also a nearly ideal subject for observing with a telescope from Earth. Venus approaches more closely to Earth in its orbit. However, Mars also passes relatively near Earth and, unlike Venus, its surface is generally not obscured by thick clouds. Mars is farther from the Sun than Earth is, so the planet often appears high in the sky. Venus, on the other hand, can never be seen far from the glare of the Sun.

Over the centuries, observers have noted various phenomena on the Martian surface, some of which they thought might be signs of life. For instance, dark markings cover about a third of the surface and change in

Mars, the most Earth-like of the planets, appears in a computer-generated image based on photographs taken by Mars Global Surveyor on a day in the northern hemisphere's summer. At the top of the globe is the northern polar ice cap, while the huge gash just below the equator is the canyon system Valles Marineris. White clouds of water ice surround the peaks of the most prominent volcanoes. **NASA/JPL/Malin Space Science Systems**

a seasonal pattern in both extent and color. They were once thought to be vast seas or areas of vegetation. A few astronomers even thought they saw straight lines that could have been canals.

The explanation of these and many other observations had to await the first exploratory space missions in the 1960s and '70s. Meanwhile, the so-called red planet captured the popular imagination as a possible home of alien life—the armies of "little green men" of science fiction stories, movies, and radio and television programs. Scientists now know that there are no manufactured canals on Mars. The changes in the dark areas result largely from dust, which shifts along with the winds. There are no humanoids on the planet, nor even any animals or plants. No forms of life have yet been found on Mars.

Nevertheless, the search for life on Mars continues, in part because it shows signs of having been wetter in the past. Water is necessary for all known forms of life. It is possible that microscopic life once existed on Mars. Today the surface is too cold and the air is too thin for liquid water to exist there for long. It is also bombarded with ultraviolet radiation from the Sun, which is very harmful to living things. (Earth's denser atmosphere protects it from most of this radiation.) If any life-form exists on Mars today, many scientists believe it would be tiny organisms in protected niches just below the surface. Whether or not Mars has ever had life, the planet remains an intriguing object of study.

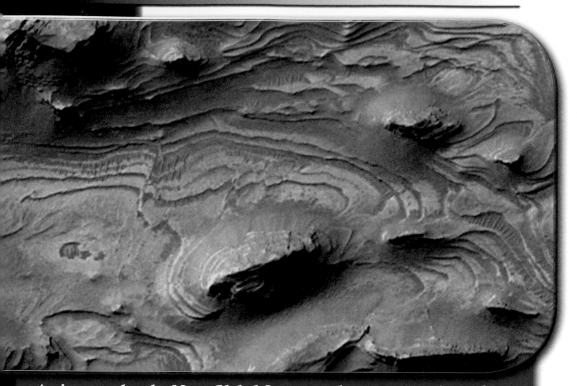

An image taken by Mars Global Surveyor shows outcroppings of sedimentary rock layers in the southwestern Candor Chasma region of the Valles Marineris canyon system. Some scientists have interpreted these formations as evidence that lakes once partially filled the canyons. **NASA/JPL/Malin Space Science Systems**

SIZE, MASS, AND DENSITY

Mars is the second smallest planet in the solar system, after Mercury. Its diameter at the equator is 4,221 miles (6,792 kilometers), which is only slightly more than half the size of Earth's. Mars's lower density makes the planet only about a 10th as massive as Earth.

In fact, Mars's density—which is about four times that of water—is closer to that of Earth's Moon than to that of the three other inner planets.

APPEARANCE FROM EARTH

Mars's distance from Earth varies considerably, from less than 35 million miles (56 million kilometers) to nearly 250 million miles (400 million kilometers). The best time to view Mars from Earth is when it is at its closest to both the Sun and Earth so that it appears both bright and large. The planet is easiest to observe when it is at opposition, or when it is on the opposite side of Earth from the Sun. Mars then appears high in Earth's sky, and its full face is lighted. Oppositions of Mars occur about every 26 months. About every 15 years Mars is both close to Earth and in opposition, an arrangement that provides optimal viewing conditions.

ORBIT AND SPIN

Mars is the outermost of the four inner planets of the solar system. Like all the planets, Mars travels around the Sun in an elliptical, or

Martian seasons

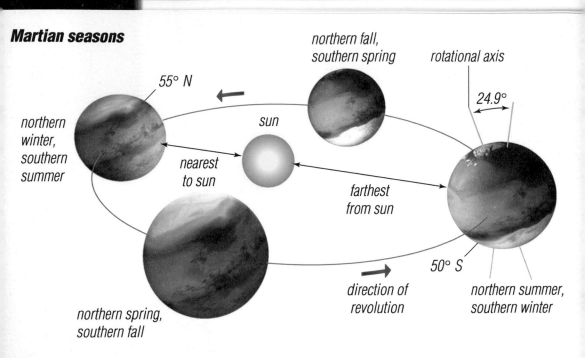

northern fall,
southern spring

rotational axis

55° N

24.9°

sun

northern
winter,
southern
summer

nearest
to sun

farthest
from sun

50° S

direction of
revolution

northern summer,
southern winter

northern spring,
southern fall

Mars's spin axis is tilted about 24.9° relative to the plane in which it orbits. As the planet travels in its orbit, first the northern hemisphere, then the southern hemisphere is tipped toward to the Sun. As a result, there are four distinct seasons on Mars. The ice caps at the poles alternately grow and shrink as the seasons change. **Encyclopædia Britannica, Inc.**

oval-shaped, orbit. Its average distance from the Sun is almost 142 million miles (228 million kilometers), which is roughly 1.5 times greater than Earth's. Mars's orbit is more eccentric, or elongated, than Earth's, however, so its distance from the Sun varies more.

THE MOONS OF MARS

Mars's two moons, Phobos and Deimos, are small and rocky. They are named after sons of the ancient Greek war god Ares (the counterpart of the Roman god Mars). Phobos means "fear" in Greek, while Deimos means "terror." They were discovered in 1877 by the astronomer Asaph Hall. Both moons are so small that their gravity is too weak to pull them into spherical shapes. Instead, they are shaped more or less like potatoes. Phobos is about 16.5 miles (27 kilometers) long at its longest point, while Deimos is only about 9.5 miles (15 kilometers) long.

Each moon takes the same amount of time to rotate once on its axis as it does to complete one orbit around Mars. This means that, like Earth's Moon, they always point the same face toward their planet. Deimos takes nearly one and a half Earth days to circle Mars, while Phobos completes about three orbits around Mars in one Earth day. Phobos is very close to Mars—within roughly 5,825 miles (9,375 kilometers) of the planet's center—and the planet's gravity draws the moon ever so slightly closer with each orbit. Astronomers think that Phobos might crash into Mars sometime in the next 100 million years. Deimos orbits Mars at about 14,575 miles (23,460 kilometers) from the planet's center and is gradually moving farther away.

The surface of Phobos is very heavily cratered and grooved. One of its craters, named

Stickney, is about half as wide as Phobos itself. The surface of Deimos appears smoother because its craters are almost buried in a layer of fine rubble. The moons reflect very little light. Phobos and Deimos may once have been asteroidlike objects that came too close to Mars and were captured by its gravity.

The Martian moons Phobos (left) and Deimos (right) are shown in photographs by the Viking orbiters. Deimos's smooth surface is contrasted with the grooved, pitted, and cratered surface of Phobos. The prominent cavity on the end of Phobos is the crater Stickney. The images are not to scale; Phobos is about 75 percent larger than its companion. National Aeronautics and Space Administration/Malin Space Science Systems

Mars is about 128 million miles (207 million kilometers) from the Sun at its perihelion, or the closest point in its orbit to the Sun. At its aphelion, its farthest point from the Sun, it is some 155 million miles (249 million kilometers) away.

The planet completes one revolution around the Sun in about 687 Earth days. In other words, a year on Mars is about 687 Earth days long. That is almost twice the time it takes Earth to complete its orbit of about 365 days.

Mars rotates on its axis at roughly the same rate as Earth. A Martian day, called a sol, lasts about 24 hours and 37 minutes, which is just a bit longer than an Earth day. Its spin axis is also tilted at an angle similar to Earth's—there is only about one degree of difference between the spin axes of the two planets. As a result, Mars has distinct seasons like Earth does. First one hemisphere, then the other receives more sunlight during the planet's orbit around the Sun. Because Mars has a more eccentric orbit than Earth's, Martian seasons are less equal in length. The Martian summer, for example, is about 16 percent longer in the north than in the south.

PHYSICAL FEATURES AND EXPLORATION OF MARS

The planet's atmosphere, or surrounding layers of gases, is not very dense. Its surface is a cold, dusty desert. It is possible that water might periodically seep up in places from ice beneath the surface. Under such conditions, however, liquid water on the surface would very quickly freeze or vaporize. But evidence suggests that in the remote past the planet may have been more Earth-like, with a thicker atmosphere and warmer surface temperatures. Large bodies of water may have been found on the Martian surface for a while in its early history. And some evidence suggests that at least some water flowed on the surface in the geologically recent past.

ATMOSPHERE

The Martian atmosphere is very thin. It exerts less than a hundredth the surface pressure of Earth's atmosphere. Like Venus' atmosphere, it consists almost entirely of carbon dioxide. Venus' atmosphere is extremely dense, however, so the total volume of

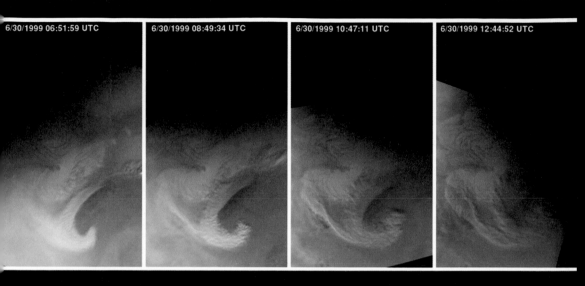

6/30/1999 06:51:59 UTC　　6/30/1999 08:49:34 UTC　　6/30/1999 10:47:11 UTC　　6/30/1999 12:44:52 UTC

Mars Global Surveyor photographed a large storm system high above Mars's north polar region. The "curl" consists mainly of water-ice clouds mixed with orange-brown dust raised from the surface by high winds. The north polar cap is seen as a spiral pattern of light and dark bands at the upper left. **NASA/JPL/Malin Space Science Systems**

carbon dioxide is much greater there. Near the surface of Mars, carbon dioxide accounts for about 95.3 percent of the atmosphere by weight. Most of the rest of the atmosphere consists of nitrogen and argon, with small amounts of oxygen, carbon monoxide, water vapor, neon, krypton, xenon, and other gases. Trace amounts of methane also have been detected. A large amount of dust particles is suspended in the gases.

The lower Martian atmosphere is roughly as cold as the air on Earth above Antarctica in the winter. It is typically about -100 °F (-70 °C). Clouds, haze, and fog are common in the air near the ground, especially over valleys, craters, volcanoes, and other areas of low or high surface elevation. Most of these low-lying clouds are formed of water ice. In

A whirlwind of dust, called a dust devil, appears in an image captured by Mars Global Surveyor. Its camera was pointed essentially straight down above the Martian surface. As the dust devil traveled, it left a faint track, at left, and cast a long shadow, at right. The dust cloud itself appears as a foreshortened white column at center. NASA/JPL/Main Space Science Systems

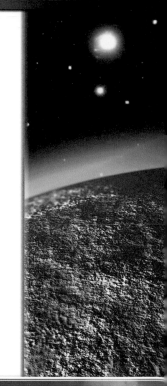

addition, very thin clouds, perhaps of carbon dioxide, are found quite high up in the atmosphere.

At the surface the winds are generally light. The average wind speeds are typically less than 4.5 miles (7.2 kilometers) per hour, though gusts sometimes blow as fast as 90 miles (144 kilometers) per hour. In winter Mars has strong jet streams like Earth's, which blow westward high in the atmosphere. These winds are much lighter during the Martian spring and summer. Unlike on Earth, the air circulation on Mars also has a fairly strong north-south pattern, which transfers air from pole to pole.

March 1999

January 200

The permanent cap of water ice at the Martian north pole appears in two images taken by Mars Global Surveyor during early summer in the north in 1999 (left) and 2001 (right). NASA/JPL/Malin Space Science Systems

Rapidly swirling columns of dust, called dust devils, have been seen whirling along the surface. Dust storms also occur frequently on the planet. They are especially common in the southern hemisphere in spring and summer, when the surface is warmest. About every two or three years, Mars is engulfed by global dust storms. Local temperature differences generate strong winds that lift dust from the surface. The thick dust clouds block the sunlight, gradually causing the surface temperatures to even out and the winds to subside. Some of the atmospheric dust is deposited in a "snowfall" of dust and ice in the polar regions.

Ice caps are found at both the north and south poles. The caps alternately grow and shrink according to seasonal changes. Each ice cap grows larger when its hemisphere experiences fall and shrinks during its spring. Most of the ice then "burns off," escaping into the air as a gas. As a result, the atmospheric pressure increases above the shrinking cap. As summer approaches, the ice cap shrinks into several small patches of ice. In fall, as gases from the air again condense and freeze to form the larger cap, the atmospheric pressure decreases over the cap.

The two caps differ somewhat in size and composition. The southern cap is larger. It

extends to about 50° S. at its greatest extent, compared with 55° N. for the northern ice cap. The north pole has a small permanent cap of water ice. It temporarily accumulates larger areas of carbon dioxide ice (or "dry ice") in fall and winter. The south pole's cap seems to contain some carbon dioxide ice and some water ice year-round (which grow and shrink seasonally).

SURFACE

The thin Martian atmosphere does not shield the surface from ultraviolet radiation from the Sun. It also does not insulate the planet as well as Earth's thicker one does. The surface of Mars is thus colder than Earth's would be if the two planets were the same distance from the Sun. The temperature of Martian air at about human height varies widely over the course of a day, from about -119 °F (-84 °C) before dawn to about -28 °F (-33 °C) in the afternoon. The temperature of the surface itself is colder. The average surface temperature is about -82 °F (-63 °C).

The rocks and soil on the Martian surface are typically rusty reddish brown because they contain much iron oxide. The planet's

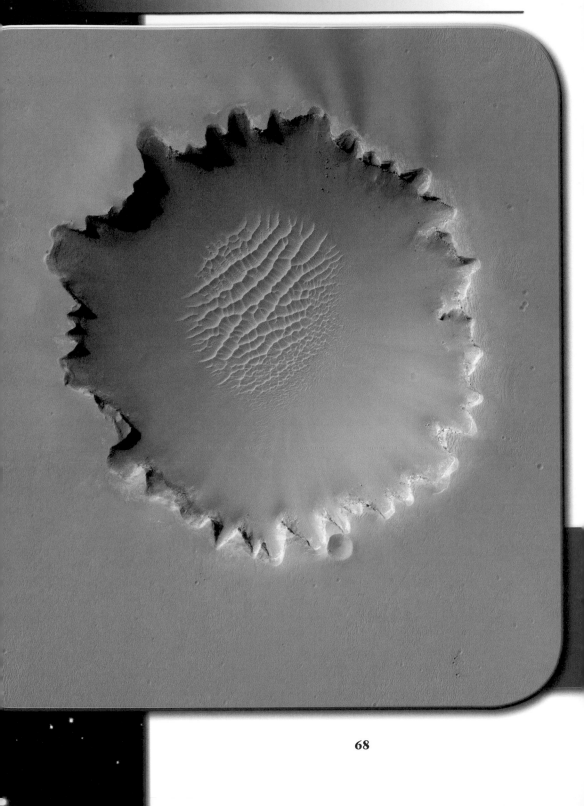

surface features include smooth, desolate plains and windblown sand dunes, deep, rugged canyons and steep cliffs, rolling hills, mesas, and enormous volcanoes. Several areas have winding channels that were probably carved by ancient floodwaters. The planet conspicuously lacks features such as long mountain chains that on Earth form by plate tectonics. Instead, many Martian features seem to have been formed by fracturing of the planet's crust, volcanic activity, or the wearing away or depositing of material by the wind.

Even though Mars is much smaller than Earth, it has a greater variation in surface elevation. The lowest point on Mars is Hellas, a giant impact basin. It is probably the result of an asteroid colliding with the planet early in Martian history. The planet's highest point is the volcano Olympus Mons. The difference in elevation between these two features is about 18 miles (29 kilometers). By comparison, on

A large Martian crater called Victoria, shown in a Mars Reconnaissance Orbiter image, has a scalloped rim from erosion and from material in the crater wall falling downward. The crater is about a half mile (800 meters) across and is located in Meridiani Planum. A large patch of sand dunes lies on the crater floor. NASA/JPL/University of Arizona

Source: Mars Orbital Laser Altimeter (MOLA) Science Team   east longitude system (used for Mars maps produced in 2002 and later)

A map of the topography of Mars shows the contrast between the heavily cratered highlands in the southern hemisphere and the smoother lowlands in the northern hemisphere. The map is a Mercator projection made with data collected by Mars Global Surveyor. The topographic relief has been color coded according to the key at right. The lowest elevations, which are colored purple, lie some 5 miles (8 kilometers) below the average reference level (similar to sea level on Earth). The highest elevations, colored white, are more than 7.5 miles (12 kilometers) above the average value. Labels identify selected major features and the landing sites of space probes. **Mars Orbiter Laser Altimeter Science Team**

Earth the difference in elevation between the lowest point (the Mariana Trench) and the highest point (Mount Everest) is some 12.4 miles (20 kilometers).

The planet's northern and southern hemispheres are strikingly different, for reasons that are not yet clear. Much of the south consists of heavily cratered highlands, while flat lowlands with few craters predominate in the north. Craters and impact basins form when asteroids or other chunks of matter crash into a planet's surface. Planetary scientists

A composite of several images taken by the Mars Pathfinder lander shows the boulder-strewn surface of Mars at Chryse Planitia. In the distance are two hills dubbed "Twin Peaks," which are about 100 feet (30 meters) tall. **NASA/JPL/Caltech**

can estimate the age of a planet's surface by counting the number of these scars. The older the surface, the more time it has potentially been exposed to falling objects and debris. In other words, surfaces with many craters are generally older than those with few craters. Earth's Moon, which is also heavily cratered, was most intensely bombarded with asteroids and large fragments before about 3.8 billion years ago. The southern surface of Mars is probably similarly ancient.

The northern lowlands of Mars are younger. They include the broad plains called Chyrse Planitia, Acidalia Planitia, and Utopia Planitia. Some scientists think that the smooth northern plains may once have been the beds of seas that were filled by large floods, but this theory remains controversial.

Some of the red planet's most prominent features lie along the borders between the northern and southern hemispheres. Among them is Tharsis, a broad, high volcanic dome covered with lava flows. Three of the planet's largest volcanoes are at the top of the dome, while Olympus Mons is just to the northwest. The largest known volcano in the solar system, Olympus Mons reaches a height of 13 miles (21 kilometers) above the average reference altitude (like sea level on Earth).

A mosaic of more than 100 photographs of Mars taken by the Viking orbiters shows the large volcanoes of the Tharsis rise, left, and the enormous canyon system named Valles Marineris, bottom center. The white bands and streaks are water-ice clouds. A. McEwen, U.S. Geological Survey

WATER ON MARS

The Martian surface today is dry and dusty. The question of whether and when liquid water has flowed on the surface of Mars is of particular interest to scientists trying to determine if life has ever existed on the planet. Liquid water is a requirement for all known forms of life. (But, of course, water does not in itself indicate the presence of living things.)

Water currently exists on Mars as small amounts of vapor in the atmosphere, as ice at the poles, and as ice in large regions just below the surface. Rivers, lakes, and even seas may

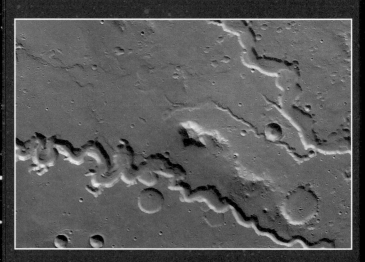

The steep-walled channel Nanedi Valles, photographed by the Mars Express spacecraft, may have formed from flowing water. It is one of many Martian valley networks that resemble river valley systems on Earth. European Space Agency

have been present on Mars in its remote past, when it was probably warmer and the atmospheric pressure higher. Several features on the surface appear to have been formed by water, either fed by rainfall or groundwater. Winding valleys on Mars look like river beds and other drainage systems on Earth. Some Martian channels appear to have been completely filled with ancient floodwaters. In addition, some Martian rocks have mineral compositions that suggest they formed through interaction with liquid water.

As mentioned above, Mars's current cold temperatures and low air pressure mean that today liquid water would not last long at the surface. However, images taken in 2000 and later by the orbiting spacecraft Mars Global Surveyor show hundreds of gullies that seemed to have formed relatively recently. These gullies appear on steep slopes in parts of the southern hemisphere. Some planetary scientists believe that the gullies were carved by water. They theorize that, episodically, small amounts of liquid water have flowed on and just below the surface in some places in geologically recent times. Moreover, pairs of images from Mars Global Surveyor that were released in 2006 show that light-toned deposits formed on two of the gullies very recently—in 1999 or later. The shape and color of the deposits suggest they may have been left by the movement of liquid water. But other planetary scientists disagree with these interpretations.

This makes the volcano more than twice as high as Earth's Mount Everest. The volcano is very broad, stretching across about 335 miles (540 kilometers). Scientists believe that Mars is almost certainly still volcanically active, though at very low levels.

The large bulge of Tharsis has stressed and cracked the surface nearby. An extensive system of fractures surrounds the dome. The largest fracture system is Valles Marineris, an enormous series of connected canyons east of Tharsis. The canyon system is about 2,500 miles (4,000 kilometers) long, which is about 20 percent of the planet's circumference. Its central depression reaches a depth of about 5.6 miles (9 kilometers), which is more than five times deeper than Earth's Grand Canyon. Sediments piled up in the canyons suggest they may once have been filled with lakes.

INTERIOR

Scientists do not have direct information about the Martian interior. Instead, they develop models of the interior based on the planet's known characteristics, such as its size, mass, rotation rate, volcanic activity, magnetic properties, and gravity signature. In addition, more than 30 meteorites that have fallen to Earth are known to have come from Mars. The chemical composition of the meteorites indicates that Mars has separated into three main layers like Earth. Earth and Mars both have a metal-rich core at the center; a large, rocky middle layer called the mantle; and an outer crust.

Mars's core is probably rich in iron and sulfur. Scientists estimate that the core has a diameter of about 1,600–2,400 miles (2,600–4,000 kilometers). Unlike most other planets, Mars has no global magnetic field. Scientists believe that fluid motions in a planet's core help generate a magnetic field, so having such a field would indicate flow in the core. It is not known whether Mars's core is currently solid or liquid. However, ancient, highly magnetized rocks in its southern hemisphere suggest that in the past Mars had a strong magnetic field, which disappeared as the planet cooled. Scientists believe that Mars is still volcanically active, so its mantle is probably still warm and in some places is undergoing melting.

Measurements of the planet's gravity indicate that the crust is thinner and denser in the northern hemisphere than in the south. The thickness of the crust is thought to vary from about only 2 miles (3 kilometers) in places just

north of the equator to more than 60 miles (90 kilometers) in southern Tharsis.

OBSERVATION AND EXPLORATION

For centuries astronomers have considered the possibility that life might exist on Mars, the most Earth-like of the planets. In 1877 the Italian astronomer Giovanni Schiaparelli described what he believed was a system of interconnecting, straight-edged channels on the planet. The American astronomer Percival Lowell popularized the idea that these features were canals that had been built by an advanced but dying Martian civilization.

The unmanned U.S. Mariner 4 spacecraft was launched on Nov. 28, 1964, and passed within about 6,117 miles (9,844 kilometers) of Mars on July 14, 1965. It returned images of the surface of Mars and transmitted information on the Martian atmosphere. NASA

Most astronomers could see no canals, however, and many doubted their reality. The controversy was finally resolved only when photographs taken by the Mariner space probes showed many craters but nothing resembling manufactured canals.

Four of the Mariner series of unmanned space probes launched by NASA investigated Mars. The first craft to successfully fly by Mars was Mariner 4, which photographed the planet as it passed by in July 1965. Its images showed heavily cratered surfaces that resemble Earth's Moon. Mariners 6 and 7 analyzed the atmosphere and captured images as they flew by Mars in July–August 1969. The first spacecraft to orbit a planet other than Earth was Mariner 9. It photographed the Martian surface for nearly a year in 1971–72, revealing widespread volcanic activity and features carved by water in the remote past.

The Soviet Union also sent a series of unmanned space probes to Mars in the 1960s and '70s. Its Mars 3 lander was the first craft to successfully soft-land on the planet, in December 1971. Unfortunately, it touched down during a global dust storm, which caused its communications systems to fail after about 20 seconds.

The Viking 2 lander (foreground) was photographed on Mars in 1976 by one of the spacecraft's own cameras. NASA/JPL

NASA's Viking probes consisted of two orbiting spacecraft and two landers. They were intended in part to search for evidence of past or present forms of life on Mars. The two landers touched down on the planet in 1976 and performed numerous experiments, including detailed chemical analyses of the Martian atmosphere and soil. No trace of complex organic material was found. A couple of experiments returned results that could have been caused by biological processes, but most scientists believe the results are better explained by nonbiological processes. In other words, though some of the results were inconclusive, they turned up no convincing signs of life on the surface near the landing sites.

The Soviet Union sent two probes, Phobos 1 and 2, to study the Martian moon Phobos in July 1988. Mission scientists lost contact with the first craft before it reached its target, but Phobos 2 successfully reached the moon in 1989. It collected data on Phobos and Mars for several days before it, too, malfunctioned.

A fairly high percentage of missions to Mars have failed, including three United States missions in the 1990s: Mars Observer, Mars Climate Orbiter, and Mars Polar Lander. Nozomi, a Japanese orbiter launched in 1998, reached Mars but then malfunctioned and could not be placed into orbit.

In addition to sending spacecraft to Mars, scientists also study meteorites that have fallen to Earth from the red planet. In 1996 a team of scientists announced that an ancient Martian meteorite contains organic matter and structures that resemble fossils of microscopic life-forms on Earth. The

The robotic rover Sojourner rolls onto the surface of Mars. The Pathfinder spacecraft captured the image after releasing the rover in 1997. **NASA/JPL**

team believed that this provided the first evidence of life on early Mars. Most other scientists have been skeptical of that analysis. There is more widespread agreement that minerals in the meteorite were deposited there by liquid water.

In July 1997 NASA's Pathfinder spacecraft landed on Mars to study the planet's geology and atmosphere. On board was a rover called

Artwork depicts the Mars Global Surveyor spacecraft orbiting Mars above the volcano named Olympus Mons. NASA/JPL/Illustration by Corby Waste

Sojourner that took photographs and collected and analyzed samples of the Martian soil. Data gathered during Pathfinder's 83 days of surface operations indicated that Mars was once more Earth-like, with a thicker atmosphere and warmer temperatures. In addition, it found surface features that were probably formed by flowing water.

In November 1996 NASA launched Mars Global Surveyor, the first in a series of orbiters designed to study the planet over longer periods. The probe began to orbit Mars in September 1997. It mapped a variety of the planet's properties, including its gravity and magnetic fields and the topography and mineral composition of the surface. It also took more than 100,000 photographs of the surface. Mars Global Surveyor collected more data about the planet than all other previous missions combined.

Several craft began exploring Mars in the early 21st century. NASA's global mapping orbiter named Mars Odyssey reached the planet in October 2001. In addition to mapping the chemical composition of the surface, the orbiter confirmed the presence of water ice just below the surface. Another mapping orbiter, NASA's Mars Reconnaissance Orbiter, arrived at the planet in March 2006 to study the climate and surface features associated with liquid water.

The European Space Agency sent its first mission to Mars in June 2003. After arriving at the planet in December of that year, the orbiter Mars Express mapped a variety of properties in the Martian atmosphere, surface, and subsurface. It found what appears to be a large frozen sea just under the Martian surface near the equator. Among the orbiter's other findings were the detection of auroras, tiny amounts of methane in the atmosphere, and both water ice and carbon dioxide ice in the southern polar ice cap. It found that the layered deposits in the south polar region contain huge amounts of water ice and are a couple of miles deep in some places.

NASA's twin Mars Exploration Rovers, named Spirit and Opportunity, landed on Mars in January 2004. The rovers collected geologic data to help determine whether the planet's environment was suitable for life in the past. By September 2006, long after its expected demise, Opportunity had traversed several miles to the large crater called Victoria. Each rover was equipped with several cameras and instruments, including a microscopic imager and a rock-grinding tool. With these data, scientists determined the rocks' mineral compositions. The rovers found several clues suggesting the past existence of liquid water on the surface.

On May 25, 2008, the U.S. probe Phoenix landed in the north polar region of Mars. One of Phoenix's most important discoveries was the existence of water ice beneath the surface in that region. The probe uncovered the ice by digging a trench with its robotic arm. Minerals, such as calcium carbonate, that form in the presence of water were also found, and the soil at the landing site was determined to be alkaline (earlier missions had detected acidic soil). Phoenix ceased transmitting to Earth on Nov. 2, 2008.

Following the Phoenix mission will be the Mars Science Laboratory (MSL). The MSL is a robotic vehicle that is designed to explore the surface of Mars and to help determine if Mars was, or is, capable of supporting life. It is scheduled for launch from Cape Canaveral in late 2011 and is planned to land on Mars in 2012.

CONCLUSION

For thousands of years, people have observed and studied the planets closest to Earth. In modern times, the invention of advanced astronomical instruments and the achievement of many successful unmanned spacecraft missions to Mercury, Venus, and Mars have led to a dramatic increase in our scientific knowledge of these planets. Even today, however, a shortage of information exists that leaves many basic questions concerning our nearest planetary neighbors unsettled. The appearance of much of the surface of Mercury is still unknown, for example. In addition, scientists continue their efforts to understand how the harsh conditions on Venus came about, which may hold important lessons about the causes of environmental change on Earth. Scientists also continue their work to determine if life has ever existed on Mars. Despite a number of observational hurdles that remain with regard to the inner planets, future exploratory space missions promise to help overcome these challenges and to unlock new discoveries about these complex and fascinating worlds.

altimeter An instrument for measuring altitude.

aurora A luminous phenomenon that consists of streamers or arches of light appearing in the upper atmosphere of a planet's magnetic polar regions.

concretion A mass of mineral matter found generally in rock of a composition different from its own.

convulsion A violent disturbance.

density The mass of a substance by unit volume.

elliptical In the shape of an ellipsis or oval.

greenhouse effect Warming of the surface and lower atmosphere of a planet (as Earth or Venus) that is caused by conversion of solar radiation into heat which remains trapped in the planet's atmosphere, warming its surface further.

inferior planet Either of the planets Mercury and Venus whose orbits lie within that of Earth.

magnetic field The portion of space near a magnetic body in which the magnetic forces can be detected.

mantle The part of the interior of a terrestrial planet that lies beneath the crust and above the central core.

phase A particular appearance or state in a regularly recurring cycle of changes.

plate tectonics A theory in geology that the lithosphere of Earth is divided into a small number of plates that float on and travel independently over the mantle.

retrograde motion Motion in a direction contrary to that of the general motion of similar bodies and especially east to west among the stars.

scarp Long, steep cliff.

seismic Of or relating to a vibration on a celestial body comparable to a seismic event on Earth, caused by an explosion or impact of a meteorite.

spectrometer An instrument used for measuring wavelengths of light.

terrestrial Belonging to the class of planets that are like Earth (as in density).

topography The configuration of a surface including its relief and the position of its natural features.

transit An eclipse that occurs when a planet moves directly between Earth and the Sun.

wavelength The distance in the line of advance of a wave from any one point to the next point of corresponding phase.

Griffith Observatory
2800 East Observatory Road
Los Angeles, CA 90027
(213) 473-0800
Web site: http://www.griffithobs.org
This observatory features a planetarium,
    telescopes, and astronomy exhibits.

Hayden Planetarium
Central Park West at 79th Street
New York, NY 10024
(212) 769-5100
Web site: http://www.haydenplanetarium.org
The planetarium operates out of the
    American Museum of Natural History
    and features exhibits and online
    resources.

H.R. Macmillan Space Centre
1100 Chestnut Street
Vancouver, BC V6J 3J9
Canada
(604) 738-7827
Web site: http://www.spacecentre.ca
The H.R. MacMillan Centre is based in
    Vancouver, Canada. The center
    inspires interest in the universe
    through programming, exhibits, and
    activities.

Royal Astronomical Society of Canada
203–4920 Dundas Street W
Toronto, ON M9A 1B7
Canada
(888) 924-7272
Web site: http://www.rasc.ca
The society offers publications, student
    resources, and programs throughout
    Canada.

The Space Place
Jet Propulsion Laboratory
Mail Stop 606-100
4800 Oak Grove Drive.
Pasadena, CA 91109
Web site: http://spaceplace.jpl.nasa.gov
NASA's Space Place was launched in
    February 1998 as a learning and commu-
    nity outreach program.

WEB SITES

Due to the changing nature of Internet links,
Rosen Educational Services has developed an
online list of Web sites related to the subject
of this book. This site is updated regularly.
Please use this link to access the list:

http://www.rosenlinks.com/tss/inne

BIBLIOGRAPHY

Elkins-Tanton, L.T. *The Sun, Mercury, and Venus* (Chelsea House, 2006).

Hartmann, W.K. *A Traveler's Guide to Mars: The Mysterious Landscapes of the Red Planet* (Workman, 2003).

Knapp, B.J. *Rocky Planets* (Grolier, 2004).

Miller, Ron. *Mars* (Twenty-First Century Books, 2006).

Miller, Ron. *Venus* (Twenty-First Century Books, 2002).

Moore, Patrick. *Venus* (Cassell, 2002).

Mortin, Oliver. *Mapping Mars: Science, Imagination, and the Birth of a World* (Picador, 2003).

Spangenburg, Ray, and Moser, Kit. *A Look at Venus* (Watts, 2001).

Squyres, S.W. *Roving Mars: Spirit, Opportunity, and the Exploration of the Red Planet* (Hyperion, 2005).

Strom, R.G., and Sprague, A.L. *Exploring Mercury: The Iron Planet* (Springer, 2003).